You Are Made Of Mornings Too

A collection of poems on falling apart,
remembering and rising again.

Kavya Ramesh

BookLeaf
Publishing

India | USA | UK

Made with ❤ on the BookLeaf Publishing Platform
www.bookleafpub.in
www.bookleafpub.com

Dedication

*To all the past versions of me that have enabled me to
get till here.
To the wind beneath my wings.
And to you, reading this. May you continue to rise,
always.*

Preface

At some point in time, life will throw something at us
that knocks us off balance.
Maybe it already has for you and so maybe that's why
you are here.

This happens to all of us, though it rarely feels that way
when we're in the thick of it.
One fine day, we wake up and realize that we can't keep
living the way we always have anymore.
Not because someone told us to change. But because the
person we have been doesn't fit anymore.
Because there's a voice inside — quieter than fear but
louder than before — whispering,
"There's more. You're meant for more."
The thing is, life isn't always gentle about handing us
these moments.
Sometimes it looks like a relationship falling apart. It
could be that a dream that didn't turn out the way we
hoped it would.
And then there are the rock bottoms. The moments that
split us right down the middle, where everything feels
like it is falling apart and its all just spiralling out of
control.
I won't tell you that it's easy. But I will tell you this-

what you choose to do with that wreckage is entirely your call.
We can rebuild something that feels like home this time.
We can grow into someone we actually want to be. And it doesn't have to happen overnight. It usually doesn't.
This book isn't here to tell you how to fix yourself.
Because I don't know how to do that and more so because you're not broken.
You are becoming.You are shedding versions of yourself that were only ever meant to carry you this far.
I wrote this because I wish I'd had something like this when I needed it most.
So much of what I have written in the following pages have come from my own journals (thank God I saved them all, no?). Pages where I bared it all. Not knowing that one day I would receive an opportunity to do this.
So, I want you to think of this book as a friend. One who knows what it's like to wonder if you'll ever find your way out. A friend who believes you already have everything you need inside you, even if you don't see it yet.
And if you are standing at the edge of something new, even if it terrifies you, I hope this reminds you that the fire isn't here destroy you. It is here to forge you. And somewhere inside all this mess, there's a beginning waiting to happen.
Whenever you're ready, you will find your way to it.

If anything you read in this book resonates, or doesn't, or
if you just have some random thoughts and memes to
share, write to me at kavyavilasini.work@gmail.com

Acknowledgements

I will be audacious enough to begin my acknowledgements by thanking myself. Because, how often do we do that? To the Kavya from primary school who decided to pick up her first book in her school library- thank you. That must have been when my love for the written word first began. I have found a safe space in every book I have read thus far and I would be nothing without them.

To my loved ones who continue to stand by me during the happy days, the I'm-so-annoyed-I-could-punch-someone-days, the I-could-really-use-some-advice-days and all the other kinds of days in between.

To the iced coffees that kept me company and the song 'Magie des fleurs' by Fjellson Weber that I had on repeat while I wrote this.

And finally, to life itself — the greatest, messiest, most beautiful teacher I could have asked for. Thank you for showing me the power of new beginnings.

The distance between you and you

For some, it happens overnight.
For others, it is more gradual.

You look in the mirror—
and a stranger looks back.

Like wearing clothes that do not fit—
too loose, too tight,
too light, too bright.
Like living in a home that no longer feels like yours,
or moving to a new city where nothing is familiar.

Except this city lives inside of you.

You are the child with wild dreams and hope,
looking in the mirror.
An adult stares back—
filled with untouched potential.
Conforming, complying, surviving.

A blueprint that was never signed off by your soul.
A life you do not recognise anymore.

Somewhere along the way, you left it all behind—
the hopes,
the dreams,
the ambition,
the desire.

Like balloons floating to the sky, one by one—
each marked with a dream you once dared to dream,
of the life you thought you would live.

Somewhere along the way,
you became fluent in forgetting.

Something inside of you went quiet.
You mistook silence for peace,
forgetting how loud your soul used to sing.

But even when you forget,
a small ember remains.
A whisper.
A hum.

It surfaces without permission.

It calls you home—
sometimes in dreams,
sometimes during breakdowns.

A new version of you lives inside you—
a version you are yet to meet.

The river must meet the ocean.
Flow gently,
or with a force
that swallows everything around it.

There is a distance now,
between you and you.

Let that distance invite you. Let that distance provoke
you. Let it be
a distance you feel excited to travel.
A journey to return—
home to yourself.

This is the part of the phoenix myth no one talks about—
the quiet ache before the fire,
the first tremor of knowing:
something must end,
because something deeper is ready to begin.

The weight that was never yours

There is a singular path
walked by countless others before us—
perhaps by countless others after us.

It hands you roles wrapped in gold.
They call it duty.
They name it love.

The obedient daughter.
The overachieving son.
Get fine grades, a job they can be proud of,
a partner who looks good on paper.
A crumbling marriage dressed as tradition,
disguised as devotion.

A checklist is passed down
that you'll spend your life ticking off—
a checklist you never approved of.

They didn't know any better,
and so they don't do better.
They followed the checklist,
and swallowed everything that wasn't on it.

You carry generations of
silence,
sacrifice,
stories that were not yours to tell,
dreams that were never yours to chase,
wounds that became yours to heal.

You wear masks stitched
with expectations and demands.
You try to fit into spaces
never built for you.

There are pre-fixed boxes for everyone.
They are black. They are white.
But you—
you are the brightest yellow,
you are the deepest red,
you are the lightest pink.
You are the whole rainbow.

How can a bird
meant to conquer the sky

be asked to swim underwater?

Adjust.
Compromise.
Fit in.
Shrink.
Sacrifice.

And so—
you perform a life you never chose,
to please the gods you never believed in.
You say yes like it's a prayer.
Wear silence like a badge of honour.
Follow footprints
that don't match yours at all.

This is the moment
when the phoenix decides
not to land,
but to burn.

You were never meant
to be the hero of everyone else's wounds.
To carry the weight of everyone else's dreams.

Take the silence and turn it into a scream.
Take the mask and build yourself wings.

Let the checklist end with you.
Let those who come after us choose their own paths,
dream their own dreams—
build a life that fits.

So
tune in to the voice within,
set fire to every 'should.'
And rise—
to meet yourself.
The weight was never yours to carry.
And neither is the shame
of setting it down.

What lives between the cracks

Piles of boxes tucked away in the attic.
Your dreams, desires, and true self
have a new address now.
No one visits them anymore—
but they wait.

You've done this for so long,
you eventually forgot it was there.
It's a distant memory that sometimes tugs at you,
like the few seconds in the morning,
caught between sleep and awake,
when thoughts don't yet make sense.

You can stuff a bag all you want,
pile the attic all you want—
but eventually, cracks appear.

Some cracks arrive like thunder
loud and dramatic.

Some barely make a sound
But they arrive nonetheless-
hairline fractures full of
half-formed prayers,
dreams that seemed impossible
desires unattainable
voices you buried
because they made others uncomfortable.

There is a moment in the phoenix's life
when the air changes.
The fire is coming
but for now it waits,
gathering its powers.

There is a lightning with your name on it.
A lightning that will strike—
not to break you,
but to break you apart
so the light can enter.

Do you have the courage
to look inside the cracks
and see clearly for the first time?
To honour what survived here—
the truths your body remembered
even when your mind forgot?

There is a version of you that lives here.
Whole.
True.
Raw.
Ready.

Nothing inside the cracks
is asking to be saved.
Only recognised.
Only witnessed.

What lives in these cracks
isn't broken—
only waiting
for the fire
to reach it.

The body that remembers

*You move through life
on autopilot—
day after day,
everything looks the same,
everything feels the same.*

*Performing inside a neat little bubble
they call the comfort zone.
And what's inside the bubble is familiar now.
It's the familiarity you crave—
even when that familiarity is toxic,
even when it has made you
unfamiliar to yourself.*

*Remember your first heartbreak?
You thought you were healing.
You told yourself you'd moved on.
And then, one day,
'that' song played.
And it all came rushing back.*

You remembered.

No—
your body remembered
what your mind thought it had forgotten
It remembered those wild dreams
you once dared to dream,
the quiet whispers of hope,
the thrill of what could be.

It remembered the tingling promise
of a future unfurling,
the soft hum of a voice
from deep within—
the one you listened to,
became one with,
if only for a moment.

You merged with that voice.
You let it speak.
You let it guide you.

Until you didn't.

But—
the body remembers

what the mind thinks it has forgotten.

Even in stillness,
the body hums—
a map of every unmet dream,
every no swallowed whole,
every moment it stayed
when everything else left.

This is the hush before the rise.
The ember just before the blaze.
The phoenix, curled within ash—
not dead, not asleep,
just listening,
just remembering.

And when the time is right,
the voice will rise.

Sometimes,
it arrives as a soft beckoning.
Other times,
it roars.

It could come as a quiet ache,
or a gut-wrenching pull,
a song carried by the wind,

a truth you can no longer ignore.

It may come just before your rock bottom—
or just after.

But come it will.
Because always,
the body remembers
what the mind thinks it has forgotten

The stories you were never told

You have inherited the hair, the nose
the laugh, the height.
But there is something else you inherited

The grief they couldn't process, the rage they
swallowed,
the dreams they buried.
The silence they did not dare break.

You were handed recipes,
jewellery,
an old photograph or two—
but the real inheritance,
that came quietly,
like dust beneath the floorboards.
A silence greatly practiced.
But this silence isn't empty- it's heavy.

It is heavy with stories you were never told.

Stories they did not know how to tell.
Of overlooked pain and unmet needs
And how their hands never fully reached
for what they truly wanted.

They speak in glory of the ones in your lineage who
survived
Yes, they were great for surviving
But they never dissect what they survived
They never speak of the joy rationed in teaspoons
so no one would call it selfish.
As if endurance is the same as peace.

You carry what was left unsaid—
the warning buried in a lullaby,
the ache behind a wedding smile,
the rage sealed shut with duty.

You feel it when you doubt your worth
without knowing why.
When you apologize
for taking up space.
When you choose safety
over aliveness, again and again.

You were never told the stories—
but still,

you live their consequences.

And now,
you're beginning to hear it—
a rustle, a whisper,
the sound of something rising
through the cracks.

That's the thing about rock bottoms—
they ask you to peel,
to sift through layers,
to meet not just yourself
but the generational echoes that shaped you.

And you realise, maybe you are the story
they never knew how to tell.

This is where the phoenix begins to stir.
in the decision to no longer carry what does not belong.
To become the first to burn clean.

Maybe it's not too late.
Maybe this is an invitation to heal not just your wounds
But also theirs.

Maybe silence is not the end
but a pause,

waiting for someone
brave enough to speak.

And maybe,
that someone
is you.

The language only you speak

There is a language
only you speak.
It was born with you—
before the world taught you
to name things.

It lives in the quiet, this language.
In the way your chest tightens
when something isn't right.
The tug in your gut
that whispers
not this, not yet, not here.

You don't know how you know—
You just do.

It hums beneath silences
It weaves itself through your dreams—
the ones that stay even after you wake,

In the dreams
you have had since childhood—
the ones that don't fade.
In the way you ache for places
that you have never been to.

It speaks in the language of longing.
In goosebumps.
In the emotions that arrive
without reason.
It's how your skin tingles
in the presence of the truth.

The world asks you
to explain yourself.
To be clearer. Louder. Simpler.
But how do you translate
the language of the soul?

No phrase
for the way light
finds you in the dark
and says—
remember? You came for this.

You've spent years
trying to silence it,

trying to fit it into something
the world could understand.

But it was never meant
to make sense to them.
It was only ever meant
to make sense to you.

It's the reason some things
just feel right,
even when you can't explain why.

It's not logic.
It's not an impulse.
It's knowing.
The kind that lives in your bones.
The kind that echoes louder
the longer it's ignored.

It is your soul's first tongue.
The sound of truth
before truth had words.

What do you think the phoenix does
just before bursting into flames?
It listens to the voice
not coming from the world

but from the inside.

And when you finally stop to listen—
not with your ears,
but with your whole self—
you hear it again.

The pulse beneath the noise.
The memory of who you were
before the world taught you
to forget.

Some truths
are not meant for everyone to understand.

And if you listen—
really listen—
you'll hear it again.

The language
only you
know how to speak.

The power of a quiet yes

It could begin with fireworks.
Or a grand declaration.
Or it could start in the quiet—
in the space between breaths,
where something inside you
Stirs awake. Fully.
Where you say yes—
not to the world,
not to the noise,
but to yourself.

A yes that barely leaves your lips,
but echoes in your chest.

A yes to rest
when you've only ever known hustle.
A yes to leaving
when staying means self-abandonment.
A yes to joy
without justification.

A yes to pleasure
without the guilt.
A yes to the version of you
that doesn't need to earn love
by shrinking.

It feels small at first.
Almost invisible.
But it changes everything.

Because that yes
becomes a seed.
It bears roots into your bones.
It finds the places you once silenced,
and begins to bloom there.

And every time you listen—
really listen—
to what you want,
to what you need,
to what you know—
the yes grows louder.

It just... stays.
Steady.
Clear.
Unapologetic.

It's a yes your being
has been waiting to say.
It's a yes that will
bring you back to life.
It's a yes that is your truth.

Just 3 letters strung together.
To make the most powerful word.
It's your spell.
Your power coming back to you.
Because this yes,
ushers in the life you're about it live—
but it's also a no
to everything you will leave behind.

The phoenix isn't told to burn.
To burn is a decision it makes
all on its own.
A yes to go up in flames.
A no remaining the same.

The moment the yes leaves your lips,
the countdown begins,
It is the RSVP
to your new life.

This yes
is also a quiet knowing—
a soul-deep belief
that you can create
your own life.

So, shout it if you must.
Demand it if you should.
But, do not seek permission.

Until one day,
you look back
and realize—
this quiet yes
was the moment
everything began to change.

Whispers beneath the ashes

When the fire has done what it came to do—
when the smoke has settled,
when everything that could crumble
has crumbled—
you find yourself
in the stillness.

Nothing looks like it used to.
Nothing feels like it used to.
Amidst the ash you sit,
your palms open,
your breathing is shallow.
You wait,
and you are not even sure for what.

It sounds like silence.
But listen closely—
it's not empty.

Something stirs.

It's faint.
Not loud, not certain.
However, it's there.
A warmth you can't quite name.
A murmur deep within your bones.

A flicker
the fire forgot to take with it.
A whisper
you almost didn't hear.

It doesn't ask you to rebuild.
Not yet.
It doesn't rush you into rising.
It simply reminds you—
you're still here.
That not everything was lost.
That something within you
survived.

Not out of resistance,
but out of love.
Out of memory.
Out of truth.

When they all thought it was over,

beneath the ashes,
buried under the rubble,
the phoenix continues
to draw its breaths.

This is not the end.
It never was.

Because even now,
beneath everything that burned,
there is something glowing.
Soft.
Steady.
Unshakeable.

It's you.
The part of you
that stayed.

The part of you
that remembers.

And when you're ready—
not before—
it will lead you forward.

Not with noise.

But with a whisper.
The kind that sounds
like your own voice,
finally returned.

You'll follow it,
not because you know the way,
but because
for the first time,
the light is coming
from within.

You are made of mornings too

You speak of your darkness
as if it's the only truth.
As if your wounds
are the only map you carry.

You forget—
you are made of mornings too.

Yes, you have weathered storms.
But you have also opened your eyes
after them.
Even now, you hold more light
than you realise.

Because you are made of mornings too.

Yes, there is dark in you.
A well of grief,
a thousand tiny deaths

you've lived through in silence.
But there is light, too—
steady, sacred,
unmoving.

You don't have to be only one thing.
You can be fire
and water.
Rage
and gentleness.
Dark night
But also, the brightest morning.

There is still life in you,
still a voice that whispers
you are not done yet.
You are the sun returning,
again and again—
even after the longest night.

Because you are made of mornings too.

Of course you will rise.
You were always going to.
Light after all, cannot be contained and you,
you carry it
in your laugh,

in your stillness,
in the way your eyes come alive
when you remember who you are.

You were never meant to stay hidden.

You are allowed to be seen.
You are allowed to take up space—
not just in survival,
but in radiance.

Let the warmth come back to your chest.
Let your yeses get louder.
Let your joy stretch its arms
and make itself at home.

Like the phoenix,
you burned,
you broke,
but now
you begin again.
Not ashes this time—
but light.

You are not waiting to become whole.
You already are.

You are not behind.
You are blooming.

You are not too much.
You are finally just enough for yourself.

This—this light in you—
it's not borrowed.
It's yours.
It always was.

So rise.
Blaze without apology.
Speak your name like it's a sunrise.
Because the truth is,

You are made of mornings too.

The sacred in-between

There is a place
you find yourself in—
not the beginning,
not the end,
just... here.

You're no longer who you were.
But you're not quite
who you're becoming either.

It's strange, isn't it?
To feel both empty and full,
lost and held,
at the same time.

You're shedding stories,
identities,
old dreams that once felt like oxygen.
And yet,
you've not grown into the new ones just yet.

This space doesn't rush you.
It doesn't demand clarity.
It only asks
that you stay.

That you keep breathing
even when nothing makes sense.
That you trust
even without a clear why.

This isn't stagnation.
This is the soil warming
beneath the surface.
This is becoming,
in slow motion.

And yes, some days will ache—
you'll wonder if you're behind,
if you're doing it wrong.
But this pause?
It's sacred.

Because in this in-between,
your roots are growing deeper.
Your voice is getting clearer.
Your light is learning how to rise.

*This is when the flames have stilled
but the fire hasn't left.
This is where the phoenix's
next rise begins.*

*Let yourself linger.
Let yourself not know.*

*One day soon,
without force,
you will feel it—
a quiet shift,
a slow unfurling.*

*And you'll realize
you never stopped becoming.
You were simply learning
how to meet yourself
more fully
than ever before.*

A thousand little risings

Not all risings look like revolution.
Some look like getting out of bed
when everything in you is asking you
to give up.
It's brushing your hair
when it feels pointless.
Answering a message.
Drinking water like it matters.
Opening the window
so the light can find you.
The daily, almost invisible acts of courage
that stitch you back together.

It's showing up
to a world that didn't pause
while you were unraveling.
It's whispering I'm here
even when you don't quite believe it yet.

You think rising is one big moment—

but really,
it's a thousand little ones.
Unseen. Uncelebrated.
But still powerful.

It's choosing rest
when guilt still clings to your pillow.
Choosing hope,
even when you can't even see it yet.

No one claps for these.
No spotlight shines here.
But they are the threads
that slowly, but surely
stitch you back together.

These are the small flames
before the fire takes shape—
the tender beginning
of the phoenix's rise.
It doesn't have to be loud
to be real.

And maybe today,
your rise looked like
getting out of bed.
Or saying no.

Or saying yes.

Maybe it looked like
staying.
Or finally walking away.

Whatever it was—
trust that it was enough.

Because the truth is:
you are rising
Not all at once.
But in your own quiet, sacred way.

And that counts.
It all counts.
It's all leading to
you being reborn
by a thousand little risings
only you will ever know.

This is where it begins

*There comes a time
when nothing blooms—
and still,
everything is alive.*

*The world doesn't always look like it's moving forward.
But below the ground,
quiet things are happening.
Powerful things are happening
Roots are deepening.
Seeds are preparing to sprout.*

*There is a season
where the trees stand bare—
not dead,
just waiting.*

*Nothing blooms all year.
Nature knows
when to lie low,*

when to gather colour,
when to press its patience
into the cold.

This is not failure.
This is the part before the rising.
The inhale before the bloom.

Because even when everything around stands bare,
somewhere underground,
a green thought is forming.

Spring doesn't rush.
It waits for its turn.
It listens
before it begins.

And maybe,
you're doing the same.

There is no medal for blooming first.
No prize for being quick with your healing.
Begin again
like the sun does—
certain of it's return
with every single dawn.

Begin again
like rain after drought—
a quiet offering to the roots
you almost forgot you had.

Begin again
as if it's the most natural thing in the world—
because it is.

You do not need to be whole to begin.
You do not need to be ready.
You only need to trust
that beginning again
is its own kind of becoming.

It is the first step to becoming.
This is not a second chance.
This is simply the next season.
Spring never forgets how to return.
The phoenix born from the ashes
doesn't just forget how to fly.
And neither will you.

Your heart knows the way

After everything you thought you had to be burns down,
you finally get to ask yourself:
what do I actually want?

It's strange.
A little terrifying.
But also... electric.

Because suddenly, you realize—
you're not carrying the old stuff anymore.
The doubts, the rules, the need to prove.

It's just you.
You and that quiet pull inside your chest
saying: this way.

No maps.
No blueprints.
Just a pulse,
a tug,

a knowing that rises up
like a new sun.

Trust the space you've made inside yourself.

There's just this:
The next right feeling.
The next brave yes.
The next step
your heart dares you to take.
And that's enough.
That has always been enough.

New beginnings can be terrifying.
Or they can be thrilling.
It depends on which story you tell yourself.
Because standing here,
at the edge of all that could be,
you are holding a kind of freedom
most people spend lifetimes searching for.

You are not lost.
You are simply unbound.

The past has been set down.
The old skin shed.
And what remains is pure possibility—

limitless,
untamed,
yours.

This is what new beginnings feel like.
A little wild.
A little holy.
Brimming with the powerful possibility of becoming.

Even the phoenix,
after the fire has passed,
lingers for a moment
in it's new skin,
stretching those wings,
feeling their strength,
tasting the new air of its becoming,
before it remembers:
oh yes,
this is what I was born for.

You are standing in that same place now.
Not who you were.
Not yet who you will become.
But ready.
Alive.
Already whole.

And your heart—wild, wise, unstoppable—
already knows the way forward
It always did.

Let the light back in

The world taught you to be afraid of the dark—
but they never said what would happen
when the dark started living inside of you.

Because they taught you to fear the dark,
you never learned
how to welcome the light and
let it merge with the light inside you.

But here's the secret:
The light was never here to shame you.

It comes quietly,
gathering in your empty spaces,
kissing the broken beams,
blessing the ruins you tried to hide.
But even darkness hungers for more.
It eats at the edges of who you were supposed to
become.
Until one day, you realize:

it isn't the dark outside you're fighting anymore.
It's the darkness within
you're finally brave enough to face.

The first time the light touches you,
you flinch.
Of course you do.
Hope feels heavier than grief when you haven't felt it in
a while.

The first time you crack open a window,
the light feels violent—
too sharp, too much.
It spills into the rooms you forgot you had.
It touches the places you told yourself didn't matter.
It shows you what's been waiting underneath all along:
the aching, electric truth of who you still are.

And yes, you'll flinch.
You'll want to slam the door shut again.
You'll tell yourself you're not ready.

But stay.
Let the light do what it was always meant to do.
Let it peel the heavy layers off your spirit,
let it pull the buried parts of you back to the surface

It's not the darkness you need to fear anymore.
It's forgetting that you were never meant to live in
hiding.

The phoenix knows this too.
Before it flies,
it lets the sun trace every ruined feather,
every scorched bone—
and only then does it remember
what it feels like to soar.
The phoenix doesn't rise shyly from the ash.
It stands there first,
wings scorched, heart pounding,
and dares the sun to find it.

This is you now.
Not a return to what was.
But a beginning of what could be.

So fling open your chest.
Let the light flood in.
You were never meant to be a locked room.
You were always meant claim the sky.

So tear down the curtains.
Kick open every door.
Let the light storm in.

Not broken, just becoming

They told you the cracks meant you were broken.
That the ache meant you were failing.
That the uncertainty meant you had lost your way.

They'll look at the ashes and call it broken.
They'll look at your timeline and call it delayed.
They'll measure your life against a checklist
and decide you're behind.

But they don't understand—
only the brave walk away from a life that doesn't fit.

Only the brave stand in the fire and say,
Let it burn.
Let it unmake me.
Let it carve me into something truer.

Because you didn't create that earlier version of yourself.
The world did.
It handed you a blueprint,

told you where to stand,
how to behave,
what to want,
who to be.

You followed it—until your soul outgrew it.
Until you could no longer fit inside a life that wasn't
made for you.
So you tore it down.
You shattered it.
You set fire to the parts of you that didn't belong.

And yes, it left you standing in ruins.
Yes, it made you question everything.
Yes, it felt like being split open.
But it didn't break you.
It freed you.

Only the brave walk away from a life that doesn't fit.
Only the brave let themselves fall apart—
not because they're weak,
but because they're wise enough to know
that growth demands surrender.

Change doesn't look graceful when you're in it.
It looks messy. Scary.
Maybe even chaotic.

*It looks like standing knee-deep in everything you once
thought you needed
and realizing you're still standing anyway.*

*The world will try to rush you.
Will try to shame your becoming.*

*But listen—
growth is not a disaster.
It is a birth.
And birth has always been a little bit wild.*

*The phoenix knows this.
It knows the fire isn't punishment—
it's permission.
It's sacred alchemy.
It doesn't mourn the ashes.
It makes them part of it's wings.
This is what makes the rise possible.*

*So let them think you're broken.
Let them wonder what went wrong.
You know the truth:
You were never breaking.
You were leaving behind what was never really yours.
You were making space for who you were always meant*

to be.
And only the brave do that on purpose.

Becoming your own safe place

No one teaches you
how to be your own shelter.
How to hold the storms
instead of waiting for someone else to build you a roof.

You were taught to search outside—
for approval, for protection, for a place to land.
You were taught to measure your worth
by how tightly someone else held you.

But this time.
lay the bricks with your own hands.
learn to speak gently to the parts of you
that once begged for rescue.
Learn to sit in the dark corners of yourself
without running away.
Build a home inside yourself,
one that never asks you to shrink to fit inside it.

It isn't easy.
Some days, it will feel like patching holes in the roof
with nothing but bare hands and stubborn hope.
Some days, it will feel like learning a new language
where every word is a kind of forgiveness.

Because yes, we crave love,
we crave safety,
we crave the feeling of being held by something greater
than ourselves.
But the minute you learn to give it to yourself—
really give it, without conditions—
everything else pales in comparison.

It's like realizing
you can plant a tiny lemon tree in your balcony,
watch it sprout under your care,
and feel more whole,
more alive,
than all the years you spent waiting for someone else
to hand you a forest.

And when you've already planted your own seeds,
when you've learned to love the sprout on your tiny
balcony,
you meet that forest differently.
Not with hunger.

Not with fear that it will disappear.
But with open hands, steady feet, and a heart that says,
"Thank you. And look - I grew something too."

It's sweeter that way.
Because you are not waiting to be saved.

You started tending to yourself
in the smallest of ways—
answering your own needs
instead of silencing them.
Listening when your body said "enough."
Holding yourself through the ache,
the doubt.

And somewhere between the first boundary
and the first brave no,
somewhere between the morning you stayed
instead of abandoning yourself again,
you started to notice:

You were becoming
your own safe place.

The phoenix knows this too.
After it rises,
It doesn't seek new lands to claim it.

It builds itself a nest from the ashes—
a sanctuary made not from fear,
but from love. Fierce yet tender.

You are doing the same.
You are becoming the place
you have always been searching for.
And this time,
no one can take it away.

Wings made of flame

You didn't just survive
the fires you walked through.
You became them.
You wore every lesson,
every scar,
every crack in your voice
like it was stitched into your skin—
not as a wound,
but as a mark of power.

They told you the flames would destroy you.
But they didn't know
you were building wings.

Not delicate things
made to flutter and falter,
but wings forged from the heat itself.
Unfolding now,
stronger for every time
you thought you wouldn't make it.

The world tried to teach you fear.
Tried to teach you to be small.
But you kept moving.
Even when your voice shook.
Even when your hands trembled.
Even when the ground gave way beneath you.

Strength is loud.
And sometimes it isn't.
It's not always fists or fury.
Sometimes, it's the quiet decision
to keep becoming
even when it would be easier to disappear.

And now—
now, you're here.
No longer carrying your past
like a chain.
No longer wearing your pain
like a second skin.
But gathering it—
weaving it—
into the wide, wild wings
you were always meant to fly with.

The phoenix doesn't just rise.

It soars.
Because it knows
every flame that touched it
was fuel.

And so it is with you.

You are not broken.
You are not less.
You are a force.
Wings made of flame,
heart made of sky,
rising not in spite of the fire—
but because of it.

Forged in fire, blooming, rising

You feared the fire would finish you.
But all it did was clear the way.

The life that will burst through now
is not fragile.
It is wild and rooted.
It knows what it cost to get here.

You will no longer grow in neat little rows,
pruned and trained by what others expected.
You are becoming a whole, riotous field of colour—
a meadow where everything is allowed to bloom,
where nothing asks permission to be beautiful.

The ash you thought would bury you
will become the richest soil.
The parts of you that survived the blaze
are the ones that were always meant to thrive.
This is not a small, cautious beginning.

*This is the kind of rebirth
that turns barren fields into wild gardens.*

*What once felt like an ending
was a clearing.
What once felt like ruin
was planting season.*

*Look at you now—
unfolding,
unapologetic,
alive.*

*You will bloom — not despite the fire.
You will bloom because of it.*

*Let the burning teach you
what dreams to water.
what parts of you
deserve to take up space.*

*You feared the fire would strip you bare.
Leave you nothing but ash.*

*And in a way, it did.
It took the versions of you
that could no longer hold the weight of who you were*

becoming.
It demanded that you let go
of every brittle dream, every hollow mask,
every smallness you once mistook for safety.

The fire wasn't your ending.
It was your forging.

Part of you refused to be extinguished,
no matter how fierce the flames.

Let your roots dig deeper.
Let your spirit grow wilder.
Let your hands remember how to build a life
not from fear, but from freedom.

You do not rise in spite of the fire.
You rise because of it.

Let yourself be remade.
Because you chose to burn,
when others would have clung to the ruins.
Because you knew, somewhere deep down,
that your becoming was worth the loss.

The phoenix does not mourn the ashes.
It does not gather what the fire consumed.

It steps forward,
wings still smoking,
eyes bright with the knowing
That its truest life only began after everything else fell
away.

This is who you must be now.
Wiser.
Fiercer.
Grace where it matters,
unyielding where it counts.

You are not the same as you were.
And that is not your tragedy—
it is your triumph.

Be the living proof
that destruction is not the opposite of growth—
it is the catalyst for it.
You were not ruined.
You were released.

And now—
Let nothing hold you back.
Let nothing keep you small.

You are the fire.

You are the rise.

The fire wasn't your ending.
It was your forging.

Rooted, radiant, and unshaken.

There will come a day
when you no longer look outside yourself for
permission.

When you no longer ask the world,
Am I enough?
because you already know.

When you stand so deep in who you are
that no passing storm can uproot you.
No stray voice can pull you off course.

You are not the winds that tear through the sky.
You are the earth itself—steady, certain, alive.

You glow from within now—
not the kind of light that desires applause,
but the kind that burns slow and sure,
lit by your own two hands,

fuelled by your own truth.

You no longer chase arrival.
You no longer apologise for taking up space.
You have become the mountain,
the river,
the steady drumbeat of your own becoming.

The world will try to rush you,
pull you back into the noise.
Let it try.
You know better now.

You know how to stay rooted
even as you soar.

The phoenix doesn't just rise into the sky—
it sinks its talons deep into the earth first.
It claims its place.
It dares to be both flame and soil.
And because of that, it cannot be shaken.

You are that rare kind of force now—
radiant because you are real,
powerful because you are planted.
Unbothered. Unbreakable.
Unapologetically alive.

You are no longer becoming.
You have arrived.

Born of love, not fear

Don't forget that the old version of you
got built in a rush—
in the middle of chaos,
before you even had a say.

You became who you needed to be
to stay safe, to be liked, to get through.
You didn't get to ask,
"Do I want this?"
You just carried on.

Maybe you became the fixer.
The achiever.
The one who never asked for too much.
The one who held it all together
even when it was never your job.
But what no one told you is—
survival isn't the same as living.

And you are here to live

a life that's fully yours
Messy.
Joyful.
Maybe it a little chaotic.
And fun.
A life that lets you experience
the full spectrum of emotions.

So this time,
build something new.
Not from pressure,
but from peace.
Not from scarcity,
but from truth.

Stop asking,
"What will they think?"
and start asking,
"What do I know to be true for me?"

Learn to stay with yourself
in moments of doubt
instead of abandoning ship.
Say,
"I'll try anyway,"
even when your voice shakes.

Let yourself rest
not because you earned it,
but because you exist.

Choose connection
not as a strategy
but as a celebration.

Stop moulding yourself
to fit rooms that don't know
how to hold you.

And slowly—
without warning—
you will begin to recognise yourself.
Not the polished version.
Not the edited one.
The real you.
The one who laughs loudly.
The one who feels deeply.
The one who doesn't need to prove anything.

Yes, fear shaped you.
But love gets to lead you home.

No armor. No mask. No performance.

Just you—
alive, awake,
and unafraid
to choose a life
that feels like yours.

Just like the phoenix
who once burned just to survive—
wingless, worn-out, crawling through the ash—
you, too, have known what it means
to live with fire as a shield.

But now—
you rise not to escape the flames,
but to fly with them.

Born again—
not of fear.
But of love.

The light has always been you

You kept searching for a sign
for something outside yourself,
a landmark, a signpost,
a voice louder than your doubt,
anything to confirm you were on the right path.

But the truth was never out there.
Not in the maps or sign boards,
not in the checklist you were handed,
neither in the stories you inherited.

It was buried within.
Under the layers you built to cope.
Under every version of yourself
you created just to be accepted.

But the truth? your truth?
It didn't vanish.
It sparked in the quiet.

It stirred in moments you almost gave up.

It lived in your restlessness,
your questions,
your refusal to settle for half-alive.
You weren't falling apart.
You were shedding what no longer fit.
You weren't off course.
You were carving your own.

And then came the remembering—
that your path was never meant to look like theirs.

What they all called delay
was always your sacred timing.

Stop living on defence.
Stop editing yourself to be understood.
Stop dimming your light
just to make others comfortable.

And during these radical acts,
you won't just remember who you were,
you will discover who you were meant to become.

This time you rise
not to prove,

but to claim.
Not to chase the light,
but to carry it forward.

And like the phoenix in its final emergence—
no longer trembling,
no longer hidden,
you don't just rise.
You soar.
Not out of survival,
but out of a deep, blazing knowing.
Wings not just born,
but built.

You carry the flame now.
You walk in your own firelight.

And this—this moment—is not the end.
It's the ignition.
Because the light?
It was never something to chase.
It has always,
always
been you.